COLLECTED POEMS
Volume I

COLLECTED POEMS
Volume I

WITHDRAWN

Michael Hartnett

Raven Arts Press / Dublin
Carcanet Press / Manchester

This book is published by

RAVEN ARTS PRESS
P.O. Box 1430
Finglas
Dublin 11
Republic of Ireland

CARCANET PRESS LTD.
208-212 Corn Exchange Buildings
Manchester M4 3BQ
England

Collected Poems, Volume I
1. Title
821'. 914

ISBN 0 906897 72 6 paper (Raven Arts Press)
0 906897 74 2 cloth (Raven Arts Press)
0 85635 568 2 paper (Carcanet Press)

Acknowledgements

The publishers would like to acknowledge the Gallery Press, The New Writers Press, The Dolmen Press and The Goldsmith Press where most of this book has already appeared in book form. They would also like to acknowledge the editors of the newspapers, periodicals and anthologies where many of these poems originally appeared, and to thank Mr. Edward Maguire for permission to reproduce his portrait.

Raven Arts Press acknowledges the financial assistance of the Arts Council (An Chomhairle Ealaíon), Dublin, Ireland.

Carcanet Press acknowledges the financial assistance of the Arts Council of Great Britain.

First published in the Republic of Ireland in 1984 by the Raven Arts Press.
First published in Great Britain in 1985 by the Carcanet Press.

Portrait of the author by Edward Maguire. Cover design by Syd Bluett. Designed by D. Bolger. Typesetting and layout by Máire Davitt (Vermilion), Clondalkin, Dublin. Printing and binding by Confidential Report Printing Ltd., Dublin. Hardback binding by Duffy Bookbinding Ltd., Dublin.

CONTENTS

For Rosemary, whom I do not deserve

brave
to keep in capture
whom he loved, this wild woman
not so old, so many years
in quiet place
unknown to all the town.
so her face was white as almond
pale as wax for lack of sunlight
blue skin by her eyes in etchings,
all her beauty now attained,
all her loveliness unwanted.
   not to say his love was lessened:
   no: he came home to her same altar
   at night, grey horse bore him to the threshold,
   quiet rooms, where the woman sang her service,
   sang to new gods, to the church of her invention
   her own cloistered psalms, in her bishoped dress of scarlet.
for she built walls to keep God in,
and waiting there from eyes ahide
at night before her tearful face
at calm crossroads her child did raise,
her child into the secret world.
   as she involved a secret Lord,
   prayed the holy prayers she made herself,
   and sang so: my Lord God is a human Lord
   not Lord of towns, but Lord of white horses, holy
   of the hyacinth, the human Lord of light, of rain.
yes, Lord of sacred anguish, hear
me, and speak in rain of trees: send
your holy fire to heat me. I
cry: my Lord of holy pain, hear.
   house of slated roof was their house
   daylight knew no way to hound them
      out of peace:
   the door was closed with iron chains
   locked safe inside an open moat
      of water:
secret in their love they lived there:
the birch-hid dove was silk with peace.

SICKROOM

Regularly I visited
since your sickness
you in the black bedroom
with the gauze of death
around you like your sheets.

Now I must be frank:
these are not roses beside you,
   nor are these grapes,
      and this is no portrait
         of your father's friend.

I know you cannot rise.
You are unable to move.
But I can see your fear,
for two wet mice
      dart
cornered in the hollows
of your head.

1958

SAD SINGING IN DARKNESS

. . . sad singing in darkness is our burden
for we have none to look to or to love.
We are lovers of rare earth: our plots
are few but flourish in the sunless angles.
No one alien for us: we have pools
to tell us who and the lipsound of stones
breaking the water is prelude to the form
that is our love. Long we gaze upon the pools,
the terrible swaying of the water:
for in these undulations is the face . . .

1958

POOR ACTAEON

Four hounds gone south,
one has your liver in his mouth.
Poor Actaeon.

You understood
her secret action in the nude.
Poor Actaeon.

The female hate
of things too female to relate.
Poor Actaeon.

A mouse, a womb
unfriendly as are life and doom.
Poor Actaeon.

Four hounds went south
one had your liver in his mouth.
Poor Actaeon.

1958

SULPHUR

Sulphur
will engulf her
or else fire:
I am Zeus and I desire
her.
My palms stir
under the electric lance.
Only the dance
of the rain
can explain
to me drop by drop
why I should stop.
Fire will encase her
and unlace her
and undo her:
I will woo her
with my sulphur
and engulf her
with my fire:
I am Zeus and I desire.

SHORT MASS
(for C.M.) 1960

listen
if I came to you, out of the wind
with only my blown dream clothing me
would you give me shelter?
for I have nothing
— or nothing the world wants.
I love you: that is all my fortune.

but I know we cannot sail without nets:
I know you cannot be exposed
however soft the wind
or however small the rain.

1

I am a vessel
black and gilt,
alive with white
cameoic figures,
and swanslender
necked.
I am a vessel,
my clay cool
to the liquid
of an untasted drink.

I do not know
my own content —
I have not searched it out:
nor have I felt
the thirstshudder
yet.

2

in the black night
of year-counting
remember me
recall my name
out of the shadows
layered like cast clothes
for I interred
all my female children
and now at every step
crushed under my heel,
the weed is
the herb the sapped stem
is crushed
under my heel
and my room's interior
is full of pungency
as if one fell
in nettles.

3

you woke to find yourself
fouled in a movement of tragedy.
you were central in harsh happenings
you were the victim, the lamb.
the demon spoke to the crowd
and made known his low violation.
faces with leaves swung into sneers
at the final disclosures.
there are no faces before us:
no reason for tongueties
— ask and receive:
I know my lines exactly.
act without audience now
approach me and speechmake;
leave me, deny me,
return and arouse me.
let us curtain ourselves:
the trees do not swing
into sneers
at our private re-actings.

4

they drag me raw
on a gravel-track.
I want no more of this.

keep me from the vast returnings . . .
returning of flesh into weals
returning of salt to my scars
returning of fears of the night
returning of pain of the gorse-gash . . .
I can be broken no more.

your torture was the torture of the cross.
you never had the solace of a public sympathy . . .
there was no darkness over the earth
and the dead did not venture forth.
you stayed quiet in your private sepulchre
and believed your body would not be your body again.
your torture was the torture of the cross.

THE LORD TAKETH AWAY
(for Eileen Lohan)

In virgin cloisters from fourteen
It was taught as the only life:
Before the body made its moves
The best wife was the spiritual wife.

They preached the convent was the bar
Between the wanted and the wild
And poured their holy lies upon
The immaculate logic of this child.

For her I wrote impotent songs,
Transparent and slight as tears,
And offered her mortal happiness
For some unspecified years.

Because for her death was
The consequence of a kiss,
While Christ, as ghostly husband,
Offered immortal bliss.

I fought, that devious lessons
Might somehow be undone,
But the odds were three to one:
Father and Son and Holy Ghost.
I had no chance against such a host.

II: Poems 1962 — 1965

DOCUMENTS FOR PAUL POTTS

I

Christ, you dared say "love"
and the Jews kicked you
through the streets to Golgotha:
the new word broke in their mouths
bitter as a wren's egg.
Impaled, you forgave your crucifiers:
they were still your people:
but your apostles skulked
in the backlanes of Jerusalem
swearing revenge.
They waited until 1933.
I heard they took your people
from the streets
and branded them with yellow stars
and railed them off to Büchenwald
in cattletrains.

II

Racialism is the last pagan cruelty and medieval satanism, the last blackness of the heart. The crooked cross of hate, the vileness of nazism, this is the same as the mind that cannot see beyond the skin into the heart.

To ask me "do you like negroes" is as meaningless as "do you like whitemen". To come nearer the answer, words like "negro", and "whiteman" must go out of common talk and into the anthropological text-books.

The negro race is dying, the white race is dying: this friction is the death-throe of the races, vicious as the death throe of the bee that will sting at the risk of disembowelling itself.

The true ûbermeusch is the monationalist, the raceless.

*"I know thee, I have found thee, and I will not let thee go.
Thou art the image of God who dwells in the darkness of Africa,
And thou art fall'n to give me life . . . "*

William Blake (From *America,* a Prophecy).

I ASKED THIS CITY

I

I asked this city
for a little thing.
My voice moved
among the alien people . . .
I asked them for a lover
— friends are of no importance
— but they had no lover,
no compatible woman.
They did not speak,
but offered me to others,
pretenders in interest
escapers from stigmas.
They offered me
aping of greatness,
unmoving music,
collective love-making . . .
but they had no compatible woman.

II

In the street
I walk among men
who are father
and women who have just
come from love-linen.
From a granite angle
over the city
I see the houses,
ironic inches of building,
dividing movement from movement,
life from life,
breaking existence up into rooms
where lust was last night
or lovelust.
The city has so many houses,
and my halfself,
hollow as a squirreled acorn,
looks down on the houses
envying the climax and fullness
in every room.

DUBLIN INFERNO

I

The canals of Dublin
are uncovered sewers.
Grey rags of swan
move between rustred wheelspokes:
whatever dies
and is not Christian
rots in the canals.
The canals of Dublin . . .
ratrippled
by slime-smooth backs:
the trees are nurtured
by the excreta
of a thousand drunks,
so walk the towpaths carefully.
Flat yellow grass
like hair blown
on an old skull
captures the filth in
the canals of Dublin.

II

Dublin . . .
the limp the grope
the gape
of the phallic cripples.
Dublin . . .
chorus of frogs
in the marsh pubs,
koax koax koax . . .
but we are not entirely lost:
a few figures tower
too high to inhale the marshgas.

Yet ask,
have you a soul?
they tell you,
koax koax koax.

III

As in a womb's sense of sterility
the desolation of the built-up area benumbs.
As if humanity were a secret
the windows betray nothing
No sound, no song:
death portrayed by dead trees:
the hands and webs of television.
The only erections are iron
and bar entrance at the street-ends
and the enclosed hugeness
encloses the little lives.
Here the windows know
this humanity should be secret

IV

The river is the conscience
of the city:
the styx between the north and south.
Eyes across the water
see the cripples and the cravings,
but to the city-stripes
and the tongues
softened and absorbed
by the suburban calm,
all evil beyond the bridge
is justified.
The snow with its holy hands
cannot blow the black nooks white.
But I am honoured:
though I live with the north,
I converse with the south.

1962

26

FOR MAIGHRÉAD DURCAN

if you walk
out of the world
in bride's clothes,
if you walk out
in white,
in bride's clothes
nothing with flesh
will wed you.

Nothing with flesh
will give you a ring
like a small gold mouth,
and your finger
will search
and find nothing.

1962

I WILL RISE WITH THE HAWK
(for John Moriarty)

I will rise with the hawk
and dive with the hawk
if you are a ringtoed dove.
If ever you should talk
again of death or love
I will believe your words.
if we are destined to be birds
then I must be one of prey
and you must be, say,
a defenseless one
symbolic of love.

I will fly into the sun
and blind you with blood.

so do not talk
of death or love:
do not even talk:
for I as a hawk
will know the haunt
of the ringtoed dove
and will decide whether
to gash the neck
or cripple the wingfeather.

1962

FIRST ANCESTRAL POEM
(for the Hartnetts "People of the Battle-Stone")

my people came upon
one who was an enemy
and with bronze blade
and sinew
shocked his skull
and cleaved it
broke it open
and bore his brain home
and limed it in secret
until it was stone-hard
and left his body
until it was naked
naked from the hunger
of the hooded crows
and they made his brain
a battle-stone
and killed his sons.

SECOND ANCESTRAL POEM

after violent taking
the air was cold . . .
my soul felt like an exposed nipple.
then I smelled my enemies' rush-floor
and the sharp hearth-smoke.
I was blinded with lime
and enclosed in a new skull.
in a leather bag
I was borne to battle
and from the salt
of my enemies' palm
to the tongue of a sling
they spun me on thongs
and flung me,
and I helplessly
split my own son's skull
imbedded his brain
and killed him.

1963

CHARLEVILLE MALL SESTINA

Woman at sad canal
clothed in a swan-cape,
lost to this water world
in green, reptile tunnels:
the white as lightning swan
swooped, and the bulrush burned.

The copper beeches burned,
the tropical canal
spun as a molten cape
of steel: locked in their world
of green violent tunnels,
woman and waning swan.

White potency of swan
that no thing female burned,
the white and pure canal,
to this undid her cape:
a new conquesting world
to her, stirred new tunnels.

Water-rats in tunnels,
an old decrepit swan,
an old hair mattress burned,
along the scummed canal:
to this her opened cape,
this legendary world.

"Look, I am naked, world,
my breasts from cloth tunnels
naked: mated by swan
whiteness, my body burned:

along this hid canal
I undid my cloth cape."

Wet swan-web on her cape,
curtsey of swan to world
of swan, to wet tunnels:
for her attempting swan
satisfaction's scar burned
her face, her hid canal.

A swan on its canal
tunnels through its wet world:
burnt, a woman's cast cape. .

1962

III: Anatomy of a Cliché

I

mo ghrá thú

with me, so you call me man,
stay: winter is harsh to us,
my self is worth no money.
but with your self spread over
me, eggs under woodcock-wings,
the grass will not be meagre:
where we walk will be white flowers.

so rare will my flesh cry out
I will not call at strange times,
we will couple when you wish:
for your womb estranges death.
jail me in this gentle land,
let you hands hold me: I am
not man until less than man.

II

te quiero

your sister, small sister,
sits: your mother's watchdog.
the dance, the dance!
can you hear the soul sing
of much love
and little bread?
an instrument
thunderous as the soul
sing pain, sing love?
the dance, the dance!
women flash like red flowers!
can I not lure your sister down
so I can kiss behind your ears
the very fragrance
of strong sweet wine?

III

je t'aime

my darling, love ends abruptly.
like a country road.
there is no time to cry, lilies
open, white and broad,
in the parks:
like delicate footsteps of spring
they quiver.
and our sad walk will bring
us to the river
and a hundred unsophisticated
girls will cry at coffee-tables:
and our sad walk will bring
us to museums
and a hundred unsophisticated
girls will wilt there, like greek fables
in marble.
look at the trees
and smile, my darling:
there is always another deceiver.

IV

Ich liebe dich

my dear,
love is a philosophical concept
one cannot love the body
for ever: the soul needs a
little affection too.
my dear,
love is a controversial subject.
we must not make love always:
we must also discuss it,
occasionally.
my dear,
love is . . . wonderful!
listen, listen
the brass band is playing
a magnificent march!

V

beside an Attic column
lure me, lead me out. although
we have built philosophies
I will honour you with sex.
go then, expect no soft words:
wine still mellows at table
and all my friends are waiting.

for all that the man achieved
will stand against you, woman:
lie with you I will, lie long:
sun the tint of ochre stone
runs in my veins: then you must
bow and cry and race me down
the long corridor of taunt.

VI

ask if I should mourn you. no:
this endless complex of snow
halves us: firs weep ice instead.
no one in so vast a land
can mourn. everyone is so
apart, in heart, in place. dead
tears become ice on my hand.

and dead faces become ice,
dead flesh takes on a crystal
coat, lonesome, loved only at
a journey-called interval.
distance of soul will kill us,
and the sky low and earth-white,
and birdcries, in frantic snow.

VII

I was sent away,
as always in this country.
piegeons rose with whistles
on their talons
and I heard you talk
a thousand times
in their sad whistlings.
'the snow is gone
the cherry trees
drop white petals
cold as snow
on my face.
O will I ever see you again?'

VIII

I will pay court to you
after an antique irish fashion,
and if you delight in singing
I will sing
and I will wake you
to uncultivated hills
where everything grows wild,
and the larks are.

> who shaped you, bore you? who
> with delicate skeletal passion
> made you and started you singing
> as you sing?
> and I wait unsure
> in the hills, afraid to start
> a deer, its head fixed far
> and its eyes mild.

for you live in a beautiful street,
in a beyond more beautiful
than I shall ever see.

IX

her iron beats
the smell of bread
from damp linen,
silver, crystal
and warm white things:
whatever bird
I used to be,
hawk or lapwing,
tern, or something
wild, fierce or shy
these birds are dead
and I come here
on tiring wings.
odours of bread . . .

X

I want you to stand with me
as a birch tree beside a thorn-tree,
I want you as a gold-green moss
close to the bark
when the winds toss
my limbs to tragedy and dark.
you are to be the loveliness
in my cold days,
the live colour in my barrenness,
the fingers that demonstrate
my ways.
I can anticipate no days
unless your graceful sway of hands
arrange my awkward life.
I want you for wife:
keep confronting me as a woman
and make this complex loneliness
more human
more alive,
and girdered by your graceful sway of hands
we shall ascend from the frigid lands.

remember we stood on the steps
one past day? remember they told
me I was God? you more than I
believed them. remember the sun
whipped the stones to a bleak whiteness
and all the suppliant people
shed themselves to a spring frenzy
like profusions of haw-blossoms?
you mistook yourself for godly
and a dwarf made your ankle bleed
with a hard horse-bone, remember?
I pursued myself to Africa
and came back to you remember?
for in your pay the senile blades
flashed a lightning down the marble
and I, your Caesar and your God
collapsed, a great red open vein
you were so sad I was not God
remember? do you remember?

XII

remember the ghosted gale? wind
older than bones shivered you, drew
so close, you came close to me and
evaded with the beauty of
musk, chamomile crushed — your flesh —
all the spirits of the sea, and
rare arms of foam frightened you close.
your body, seasoft, insistent.

into Dublin in a lovely dawn,
the exaltation of something beautiful
being captured, brought ashore,
fanned pinions of some white gull
or some indefinable seabird,
into Dublin, you,
hands cold on the steel rail
like ivory spiders,
and above you, all your race
immaculate gulls, virgin in this lovely dawn,
shrieking the battled ship
into the weed-embroidered pier,
into the bay,
into Dublin in a lovely dawn.

all we have stood to gain by poetry,
all to be gained by the colossal exercise
of music, all to be gained by gazing
at the finer geological ventures,
the vicious and eternal embrace
of spray breaking into a thousand
kind of lightnings against limestone,
are made small as a crushed flower
when we find that we can resurrect,
seahigh as any headland,
such a fighting, breaking into lightning
love, love as phoenix as the sea itself.

you, some elegant shored bird
tern or skua, hardly a bird —
a cloth of tight foam,
a comb of slight haze,
hovered and alighted on flesh
like a woman
over the coloured pools
of the many and amazing flowers
and whorls of gold weed
fernhair, webs, lace,
pearled ribs of marine ghosts
landed on my hand a second
eyed my eyes with your wild sea-eyes
fluttered,
      and flew back
      into your world of whirl and wave.

Ireland is the woman we love,
or if we love less patient beings
we set them against her landscape,
measure their grace beside her trees
see if they become the salt-white mist
ever caressing her many breasts:
Ireland is the woman we love:
all our loves are synonymous
with her: nor have they her art
to seduce, embrace, betray
and in her many-folded veils
to stand on her limestone loins
and call 'come back come back
suckle my many breasts
bring all you love, build all you would
I will devour you all
and vomit you all up
and you will love me
and dream of my many breasts
and bring back your loves
to sleep in beds you share with me,
my potent ghost in all your dreams.
who is that woman who turns your head?
Ireland is the woman you love'.

XV

moon says it is so late,
lovely to leave, I cannot
go from you
nor this etching in moon by stealth,
this picture of yourself,
can I leave it: bats that skulk
the sky and fault
the lunar hand, do not untrue
moon-stroked narcissus:
what flowers are light-locked now
are in a soul no flowers failing
in black bat-shadow . . .

so vast, the petal wields
a lovely touch of light,
you are vast as petals
self-yielding in great calm
faulting all for loving less,
more true and vast than the vast
narcissus flower
infinite in its woodlocked soul,
small and infinite as you . . .

so lovely you,
that loving by yourself
is not a fault,
you are the true narcissus
loving what is loved in you,
the love of lovers:
you are the true narcissus,
flower-in-soul.

XVI

some white academy of grace
taught her to dance in perfect ways:
neck, as locked lily, is not wan
on this great, undulating bird.

are they indeed your soul, those hands,
as frantic as lace in a wind,
forever unable to fly
from the beauty of your body?

and if they dance, your five white fawns,
walking lawns of your spoken word,
what may I do but let linger
my eyes on each luminous bone?

your hands . . . are music and phrases
escape your fingers as they move,
and make the unmappable lands
quiet orchestra of your limbs.

for I have seen your hands in fields
and I called them fluted flowers
such as the lily is, before
it unleashes its starwhite life:

I have seen your fingernail cut
the sky and called it the new moon . . .

XVII

it was a new and pagan dawn,
and gods in quiet museums
turned their antique eyes to the snow
around Paraeus.
and electric Zeus
roared ice, and Pan danced,
and the old music of the old gods
trilled marble octaves
through the Athens streets,
and the cypress woke,
sombre on the Acropolis,
and the Attic hills
rushed inland, their wake
an undulating whirl
of starlings and white smoke:
and the cypress sang.

white waists of women
were the frantic trees,
and branches, human
immaculate hands:
and there was a river laughter
and a wild talking in treegroves
and strange voices by deserted pools.
came ashore, her shell an italian ship,
her foam the spring snow, an Aphrodite:
and the bees to the honey that came from
the sea, pointed their strange directive dance.
cypress-slender on the Acropolis
she walked, through the rows of welcoming gods,
quiet: her hair side-tressed to show one ear,
so white, a marble immobile beauty,
still as the untenanted Parthenon.

Athens 1967

49

I THINK SOMETIMES

I think sometimes
    of the fingernail slotted
    to most sensitive red flesh.
I think of it
    ripped out, broken and made raw
    with a bone-contracting pain.
Naked, bleeding,
    white concave of hard dermis
    and its red, moist groove of pain.
              Death or going
away of you is all this,
the break of a fingernail
              from a finger,
your mooncapped fingers lucid
to blood beneath, my own blood,
            Oh my sweet wife!

: Thirteen poems written in Madrid 1964

(i.m.F.G.L.)

1

All that is left and definite
is the skull:
the dull fibres and flesh are gone.
the long femur survives perhaps,
or the wreck of ribs,
but nothing plasmic.
No alien could figure how it loved,
longed to avoid death.
He could perhaps by reconstruction
see it stood,
see, if the tarsals were intact,
it fled, it grasped.
but how could sight be guessed at,
the eye-bowls empty?
How could he envision blood,
arteries and heart
flaked down and dusted?
Or hair, wave-long and starred,
that sparkled out under fingers,
under amber?
He could not.
All that is left and definite
is the skull full of cockroaches,
and hollow fragile strand in twos
rayed like tendrils
out about a root.

2

Only a boy, Narcissu,
only a boy,
virgin as apples
before windfall,
singing in twilight
as we all sing.
Do not love him
because he has your face:
do not taint him.
Let him choose himself
endless shifting from lover to lover,
or the task of procreation
that he considers vile.
Let him find himself
as we all found ourselves,
tortured by our choice,
or crucified by our alternative.
No one wants to share your hell:
let them make their own.
For we have heard a myth
in Western Europe,
That there are some men
who take women as wives.

3

Bats, the cemetery yewtrees,
pylongs, and nightwalkers,
along the river
like arbitary figures in abstract.
No eyes dart down,
no hesitance in pace:
these people are uncomplexed
or else at night
their rooms dance to riots
of wide limbs.
For her,
breasts bound with fish grace,
pirouettes at hand-end,
and are exposed,
nipples erect as a child's fingertip,
and pink, not like roses,
pink as some senstive underskin.
and no eyes dart down,
and no one hesitates.

Is it possible
a young woman
can breastfeed
on a riverseat
and not arouse me?

4

Her diadem, pain, taut lines on the skin-surface,
and her eyes forever enfiguring tragedy . . .
I knew she had her own life
and we were both too dedicated to our arts
to be dedicated to each other.
I knew that her upheaval was violent
when she chose corruption, chose to be vainglorious.
But as I am cold, it took no violence in my soul
to cease to sympathize.
Now when we meet (and we meet often,
perhaps we *do* fear each other)
we clash intellect with memory,
and she never wins.
but once she won, and left me mortal
by a simple act: in company I met her
after months: she was the honoured,
her poetry had enthralled
she saw me and she
(she and I who had laid naked body
to naked body, times before,
she and I who made a point
of being familiar with nipple, groin
and marking so we might never *fully* part)
— she saw me and she
shook my hand.

5

Rimmed as ponds are,
the eyes are rimmed . . .
aquatic weeds,
the green light fluid down,
thorax of a drowning wasp:
speared on follicles
the weighing dew aching for its silt
downdrawing to the (chrysalis-
glittered) beds, the stacked
and debrised cells of larvae . . .
belled as flowers are,
eyes are belled . . .
cupolas draw wasps:
hooked pollen now is parasitic
and flies the tintless world
and settles safe, with none of gratitude.
Then through crude olfaction
vague encouraging lures them
here to syrup
caught in oystered flowers
green as leaflight,
the risen teeth blurred with honey:
and as the first drop drugs,
the walls lock, the luring syrup
now is acid and works disintegration . . .
yes, eyes are similar . . .

6 EL RETIRO

As in a roman garden,
this fantasy in seconds heals me,
hedges hewn as if in quartz,
laurel-leaves wax-winking in the sun,
the fountains spuming amber,
granite seats with stone-blossomed arms,
and the carp pools, and the minnows
like fine copper needles,
like cloth-of-gold fringes,
as in a roman garden.

No toga, no bond-woman,
no flute-music, but beyond
the collonades, the lions roar
and the vixens yip in their cages
and all the birds of Asia and Africa
are trapped and beautiful.
And a vague and feeble senator
with botanic leanings, has paled in
all the flowers of Asia and Africa,
as in a Roman garden.

Between the citizens and free-men,
bidden at their callings
recording their speech,
the brilliant, the inane,
by the laurels, mono-gifted
sits a scribe, a slave,
as in a roman garden.

My mind demands in bulk
what the brain can only give
in measured pieces,
its brutal hounding after poems,
its dream, by these to gain affection,
to gain the critic's kiss of death.
Dream, to raise my father,
raise him up,
from his many calvary-falls.
And if it is power to no more be laughed at,
I want this power.
I want this power —
more than I want a woman,
more than I want the children
who would have my eyes, her beauty.
but I am shaving a limited beam,
honing it down to fragility:
neurones flock from me like dandruff:
imbecility, death, await the carpenter.
I am picking my own hands raw,
sucking my eyes my marrow out:
nothing is sourer than my own liver:
but I gnaw, I gnaw.
What was art became habit
and the habit became ritual
and the ritual became fanaticism:
if ever a man made a devilpact, I did.

8

Poor sailor who no more
can venture hazards,
safe in chrome and captainship:
weak was your flight to difference,
your run away from bus-stop,
briefcase and security.
Be rule to me
who wish for cumuli,
for wind be-coneshaped clouds,
for captaincy,
for countries where the soul
migrates, at once becomes
a castaway,
an outcast
lost in language and experience.
As the horsehoof gathers stilts of snow
in winter,
the shoesoles gather stilts of earth
in domicle:
we cannot cast away our gatherings.
The past is a vile smell
we cannot wash.
We are as naive as our sins,
as seashore rocks
that press for integration
and only repel, only embrace
the sea.

9

There are pools and pools, Narcissus.
a window is a pool,
a mirror is a pool.
In the days that droop,
that lag like sickness,
after you think, before you act,
you surely see your face.

(outside the window.)

Outside, short and darkhaired,
a man reads a magazine:
he is surely you.
Mark the look of fear,
the agony after the book reviews —
even this has a last page.

Or worse, the mirror,
hung perhaps, you argue,
at such an optic inclination,
that suddenly in the morning
you look and do not see your face.
But you are afraid
of this vampiric privilege:
surely the mirror is defective.
My, Narcissus,
your face of the present
implements nausea:
there are pools and pools.

If it rain,
then let it rain
sulphur, fire and fall-out
all the legendary stone
in fluid form.
bare them to the bone,
the street-stragglers,
flesh open like earth ploughed,
the white rock of bone
drying to the air.
Let the rain allow them no screams,
let their deaths be dignified.
And if the flash of heaven flash,
let their shadows,
their most valid parts,
blacken the walls,
dignified and upright,
at last, in spite of life.
And if they live
or if their seed survive
let their mutant offspring walk,
however humped,
however multidigital,
dignified and upright,
in spite of life,
at last, in spite of civilization.

11

Whoever does me kindness,
he shall come in:
I do not know the bent of crimeful minds,
nor conscience,
nor do I want a soul's graph.
Whether guilty
before god or principle
I do not care.
A night I would have slept
in torment, under frost and hunger,
you said: "I have a bed
in which you shall owe fealty
to no partner, female or male condition,
it is free for sleep, for heat:
and in the morning I shall give you food."
Only a race, a group,
or a mind that bids a group
can utter condemnation,
but not I.
My friends are all that nourished me,
and if they are in flight
from law, from conscience or from men,
whoever has done me kindness,
my house is his:
he shall come in.

12 *for Enrique Arias Real*

It is nine of the night.
the bats swerve from the winesmells
and the garlic-mouthed aliens
talk unintelligibly.
about me, no doubt,
my close-cut hair, my corduroy.

The women wallow in pregnancy,
intoxicate their children with affection:
prosperity, prosperity!
— at the expense of truth.
I hate this country.
I hate the joy, the loquacity,
the blind and crippled given compensation
as match-sellers, ticket-purveyors,
the illogic of the people
building again after war
and expecting another:
and the police,
the police, the military, everywhere
like rats that dominate
a refuse-heap
when it is too dark for crows.

He is dying, the coin-adorner,
and he will be mourned
and what are principles in face
of cheap wine, cheap cigarettes?

on every wall a window
the king has writ these words:
"25 años de PAZ".

All we have before us
are permutations
of art, architecture
and poetry.
The gods have been
and made the rules.
And I am not afraid
to admit the threshings
of an anaemic state of order.
We need new blood
but where is it to come from?
The deprivations of the negro,
the hope of blending the cultures
of so many stone-age nations?
What is to run in the veins
of Pharaoh, Caesar, Socrates?
There is no blood worthy:
we need the compulsory intermarriage
of a new planet,
or if we could cultivate
a planet to think
what new proseforms, verseforms,
what forms of art and architecture
we could enjoy!
Say it now, last will of the white myth,
we must lay ourselves down
and admit we are exhausted.

October 1964

V: Poems 1966 — 1970

BESIDE THE VULGAR CHAIRS

beside the vulgar chairs,
the matted lace
of the reign of George the sixth
a woman on a balcony across
lacerates her face.
beside the moss
in potted soil
she and an old man wait
charitable bread
in silver foil
from the charitable state.

I should have married
in my early years
a Cumberland shepherd
with winking shears,
and lived where sparrows
are extinct.

"YES," SHE SCREAMED...

"yes," she screamed, "call me no good!"
and she became hysterical
and killed herself.
at a deliverance up of death,
the shamed pelvis
unburdened itself of a stillborn,
and then the mouths angry at fate,
the angry hands
lit up in the room, outpushing the walls:
and the curtains, old oilglobes and chinese bowls
stoods, ears open,
and absorbed the overtones.

after a hundred years,
on a similar night,
a new couple aired a petty disagreement
and the curtains, old oilglobes and chinese bowls
stood, mouths open,
at the similar chord of circumstance struck,
a wraith, transparent, obviously female
beat the floor,
and before the cowering couple
"yes", she screamed, "call me no good!"
and she became hysterical
and killed herself.

this friend, an old man
bearing slow gentility
with his crippled walk
and smell of senility
moved among his treasures,
tusks and lyres from India
wooden masks from Africa,
and shook and smiled and spittled.
spiked iron waved before my face.
"this is a norman mace", he said.
and the old man
bearing slow gentility
swung it violently
and killed me,
bone insplintering my brain.
lit with no surprise
soft upon the floor my eyes
fell out.

"DON'T GO," THEY SAID...

"don't go," they said,
"the night will be dark,
the road white with rain
and you will lie there,
eyes close to a reflected light
and wonder 'am I dead?' "
        and I will be dead.
metallic form no longer form
nor the body a body,
twisted into death:
and trapped there,
not knowing whether that shape
smelling of blood and rain
is still a body or something dead:
and at the first sound,
perhaps a fall of split glass,
you will remember and breathe,
all the entire uselessness of your life
in a fearful rhetorical monosyllable,
"yes?"
and a huge black bird
will rise in flight on its quiet wings.

no, that cell is for maniacs . . .
this one we keep unlocked,
for here is a gentle man tending ferns,
to whom there is no world
but the mute fern world,
where all is green and delicate
and there is no strife,
save the stems thrusting the earth
the spore being loosed on the air
in silence, and coming to ground
as silently . . .
we do not allow him a trowel:
you notice he breaks the loam
with his fingers.
do not attempt conversation:
he will ignore you.
there is no voice for him
but the fern-arms gentling to the window.
It is so foamed with green lace here
that we call his room
"the green tapestried room".

I HAVE EXHAUSTED THE
DELIGHTED RANGE...

I have exhausted the delighted range
of small birds, and now, a new end to pain
makes a mirage of what I wished my life.
torture, immediate to me, is strange:
all that is left of the organs remain
in an anaesthetic of unbelief.

coerced by trivia, nothing to gain
but now, or to be pleased through one long night

and forsake instead something immortal?
and the graceless heron is killed in flight
and falls like a lopped flower into the stalks.

small birds, small poems, are not immortal:
nor, however passed is one intense night:
there is no time now for my dream of hawks.

I WAS VOLCANIC

I was volcanic
and the mystic eye:
I was alchemist,
making all base, gold.
I was fantastic
warlock of the world.
When came my poems
they spat like pollen,
or many loosed birds.
I, ring in water
that made many rings:
I, taxidermist,
hung my images
in dull rooms,
lit in my own light.
I could name grasses
and five kinds of rose.
what chervil was, I
knew: a dread of tern,
cranesbill, camomile.

and now,
the owls come back,
the horsehair owls,
the fox, the dove,
the blacksparred sparrow-hawk.
they thud in balls of fur,
come back, fly down, recur:
the old names taunt me
in a long, dry haunt.

I HAVE HEARD THEM KNOCK...

I have heard them knock
on my dimension
like chimes of glass on glass
or one water-drop
falling a long unlit way
into a deep well,
       but I have never known
       the eternal word for "enter".

And they have loosed
melodic pulses in my ears
like cut-glass pendants
struck by fine steel needles,
       but I have never known
       the eternal word for "yes".

And moods from their tangent world
have urged me in,
talked me my mind a tapestry
with one flaw,
that flaw the way I can come in
and live their chiming world,
       but I have never known
       the eternal word for "open".

I HAVE MANAGED...

I have managed to keep
hysteria at arm's length;
I have managed to sleep,
and wake with a partial strength
undone at the first door
I knock on that very day,
begging an editor
for some literary pay.
I have suppressed a scream
in an empty cinema:
celluloid its thousandth ream
not kept the hounds at bay.
and within such strictures
the heart survives
and learns to live
with second-rate pictures
and second-rate hysteria.
And within such strictures
I have a second-rate heart
finding itself in a minor part,
knowing what it is to be loved
and not love back with equal strength.
Still, I have kept hysteria
at arm's length.

I heard him whistle
in the night-frost,
delicate waterbirds:
your otter, meshed
in crochet moss.
I shot him dead —
sudden fire and smoke,
crackles of moonlight
from my rifle,
rain from erupted water
made a small rain back
and the echo batted
along the hills, a ball
on the hollow floor
of an above room.
I sat in the shallows
crying, eating
the vital parts
of a trout:
and with a knife
unslit the skin
between
my webbed fingers.

FAIRVIEW PARK: 6 a.m.
(for Dan McMahon)

I

Night into a trumpet-mouth
had funnelled,
loudly in silver to the east and south:
in viscous drops light had tunnelled
into a sudden scar of blue.
An audacious blackbird started,
and the cock crew.
A young lady,
vague in nineteenth-century dress,
massive and locked with lace,
her oaken-old, her lily face
stretched with nineteenth-century stress,
had clasped my wrist.
She was obviously out of place,
obviously distressed.
"It is not as if we parted,
— indeed we never met,
but who shares my dawn with me
must not forget
the trees are brokenhearted."
I fumbled with some careful words,
having no muse at hand.
She flew, a flock of migrant birds,
across the wailing land.

I spoke to a lone plover
in no uncertain fashion
"What feather of a lover
do you seek with such passion?"

Its piebald, reptile glance
marbly regarded me.
Its plumed, nunlike stance
disconcerted me.

"Can you not see the female curve
beneath this down.
nor in this birdlike frown
detect a moving nerve?"

It clawed me, shrieking, human,
and fled across the park,
Perhaps the internecine dark
made it a running woman.

1969

base to the smaller
words of god, always
bees, the ears could hear
in the country land
the incessant bees,
mouse on most fragile
leaves walking; ripe noise
of apples, seeded
heads of grass shook like
small infinite beads,
rats in water sank,
barks of distant dogs.
there was a land once
where ears were idle,
the river pursed lips
over fish for flies,
the soft pipistrelle,
where candlelight cried
where ears heard owls fly,
where ears were all eyes,
where ears were idle.

THERE WILL BE A TALKING

There will be a talking of lovely things
there will be cognizance of the seasons,
there will be men who know the flights of birds,
in new days there will be love for women:
we will walk the balance of artistry.
And things will have a middle and an end,
and be loved because being beautiful.
Who in a walk will find a lasting vase
depicting dance and hold it in his hands
and sell it then? No man on the new earth
will barter with malice nor make of stone
a hollowed riddle: for art will be art,
the freak, the rare no longer commonplace:
there will be a going back to the laws.

A SMALL FARM

All the perversions of the soul
I learnt on a small farm.
How to do the neighbours harm
by magic, how to hate.
I was abandoned to their tragedies,
minor but unhealing:
bitterness over boggy land,
casual stealing of crops,
venomous cardgames
across swearing tables,
a little music on the road,
a little peace in decrepit stables.
Here were rosarybeads,
a bleeding face,
the glinting doors
that did encase
their cutler needs,
their plates, their knives,
the cracked calendars
of their lives.

I was abandoned to their tragedies
and began to count the birds,
to deduct secrets in the kitchen cold
and to avoid among my nameless weeds
the civil war of that household.

CROSSING THE IRON BRIDGE

"My dear brethren, boys and girls, today is a glorious day!
Here we have a hundred lambs of our flock, the cream of
the town, about to receive the Body and Blood of Christ,
about to become Children of God, and to enter into a
miraculous Union with Jesus . . .

> Into the cobweb-coloured light,
> my arms in white rosettes,
> I walked up Maiden Street
> across the Iron Bridge
> to seek my Christ.

"It will be a wonderful moment when the very Body and
Blood of Our Lord Jesus Christ is placed upon your
tongues — what joy there will be in Heaven! So many
valuable little souls safely into the Fold! Look behind
the Altar! There will be angels there, ascending and
descending, singing songs of joy . . . "

> Into the incense-coloured light
> my arms in white rosettes,
> I walked the marbled floor
> apast parental eyes
> to seek my Christ.

"Christ will be standing there in all His Glory, his Virgin
Mother will smile and there will be a great singing in
Heaven . . . "

> Under the gilded candle-light,
> my arms in white rosettes,
> my mouth enclosed my God,
> I waited at the rail
> to find my Christ

"There will be the glow of God in your veins, your souls
will be at one with Heaven: if you were to die today,
angels would open the Gates of Paradise, and with great
rejoicing bear you in . . .

Back to the human-hampered light,
my arms in white rosettes,
I walked: my faith was dead.
Instead of glory on my tongue
there was the taste of bread.

VI: Wake Poems

MAIDEN STREET WAKE

I watched the hand
until a finger moved
and veins above the index knuckle
pulsed.
That was his last movement.
She had a band
of tan tobacco juice
upon her chin. Her few teeth buckled.
That was all the grief that showed.
In public.

Columned and black with women in shawls,
yellow and pillared with penny candles,
bright-eyed and blue-toed with children
in their summer sandals,
that was the mud house, talkative and lit.
In the bed, the breeding ground and cot,
he wore his best blouse
and would have seen
the finest teacups in his life.
But he was white
as an alabaster Christ,
and cold to kiss.
We shuffled round and waited.
Our respects were paid.
And then we ate soft biscuits
and drank lemonade.

MAIDEN STREET
(for Dennis Deere)

Full of stolen autumn apples
we watched the tinkers fight it out,
the cause, a woman or a horse:
Games came in their seasons,
horseshoes, bowling, cracking nuts,
Sceilg, marbles — frozen knuckled,
Bonfire Night, the skipping-rope
and small voices on the golden road
at this infant incantation:
  "There's a lady from the mountains
  Who she is I cannot tell,
  All she wants is gold and silver
  And a fine young gentleman".

We could make epics with our coloured chalks
traced in simple rainbows on the road,
or hunt the dreaded crawfish in the weeds
sunk in galleons of glass and rust,
or make unknown incursions on a walk
killing tribes of ragworth that were yellow-browed:
we were such golden children, never to be dust
singing in the street alive and loud:
  "There's a lady from the mountains
  Who she is I cannot tell,
  All she wants is gold and silver
  And a fine young gentleman".

EPITAPH FOR JOHN KELLY, BLACKSMITH

Black clothes do not make mourners:
    the cries come out of the heart.
And local men at street corners,
    who have stood
    and watched grained wood
in horse-hearse and motor-hearse,
    white plumes of feathers, blue plumes
of smoke, to the dead man's part
    of town, to the rain-dumbed tombs
to, talk his life, chapter and verse,
and of the dead say nothing but good.

    In Maiden Street
    what man will
    forget his iron anvil,
    an early Monday morning, sweet
    as money falling on the footpath flags?

ALL THE DEATH-ROOM
NEEDS
(for David Marcus)

all the death-room needs,
long hair in silver
spiralled and unbright:
shadows of the eyes,
finest lace: finest
wax and candles and
finest wax the face,
the gnarled horn beads
about the lax hand.
The priest in passion
for the dead, his soft
hands and quiet sounds
deathbed linen kept.
And the ritual
of prayer: and cries:
and Christ's chrism.

THE NIGHT BEFORE PATRICIA'S FUNERAL...

the night before Patricia's funeral in 1951,
I stayed up late talking to my father.

how goes the night, boy?
    the moon is down:
    dark is the town
    in the nightfall.
how goes the night, boy?
    soon is her funeral,
    her small white burial.
she was my threeyears child,
her honey hair, her eyes
small ovals of thrush-eggs.
how goes the night, boy?
    it is late: lace
    at the window
    blows back in the wind.
how goes the night, boy?
    — Oh, my poor white fawn!
how goes the night, boy?
    it is dawn.

FOR MY GRANDMOTHER,
BRIDGET HALPIN

Maybe morning lightens over
the coldest time in all the day,
but not for you: a bird's hover,
seabird, blackbird, or bird of prey,
was rain, or death, or lost cattle:
the day's warning, the red plovers
so etched and small in clouded sky
was book to you, and true bible.
you died in utter loneliness,
your acres left to the childless.
You never saw the animals
of God, and the flower under
your feet: and the trees change a leaf:
and the red fur of a fox on
a quiet evening: and the long
birches falling down the hillside.

PRAYER AT DEATH

what was not human
though from womb of woman,
for this, a small grief.
for whom forced a love
on you, will have to be
the necessary funeral,
the necessary grief.
for you, already
skeletal, you have sinned
by forcing years of
faithfulness from us,
die now, rest: let us rest.

there will be valid
human grief for all
these deaths: the heart will love
all it has to love.

FOR EDWARD HARNETT
born October twelvth, 1942
died November twentyninth, 1942

I

Birds cross
the lunar apex
and cry down
the saltmade balconies of stone:
his voice from bill of seamew,
caved in his limbo,
Edward.
That I should mourn, he speaks
out of the earth he has become,
his sound
the echo of his longing to be here.
every gathering of branch and cliff
star and wingclip
calls him here,
implies his absence:
I have borrowed his life
and perhaps, his poetry.

II

We are alone:
toned by rock
the wind gesticulates
and white by moon
the sea throws up its arms.
We are alone
because the dead are alone.

VII: Notes on my Contemporaries 1969

PROLOGUE

Pardon my omissions: there
are a hundred names unsung,
sad saints I have excluded,
the kindly hundred men gunned
down by malice in public
places, made despicable
by the cold critic and clique:
laughed at, drunk for weeks: unable
to prosper in other's art,
unable to report their own
neglected business well:
orphaned by no will for home.
For I mean the hangers-on,
the beer-buyers, song-lovers,
idolators and tavern clowns,
the poor fools put down lower
by low men whose art is dead,
hoping in their stead no song
will come from those they half love
and half hate, and prove them wrong.

THE POET DOWN

He sits between the doctor and the law.
Neither can help. Barbiturate in paw
one, whiskey in paw two, a dying man:
the poet down, and his fell caravan.
They laugh and they mistake the lash that lurks
in his tongue for the honey of his works.
The poet is at bay, the hounds baying,
dig his grave with careful kindness, saying:
"Another whiskey, and make it a large one!"
Priests within, acolytes at the margin
the red impaled bull's roar must fascinate —
they love the dead, the living man they hate.
They were designing monuments — in case —
and making furtive sketches of his face,
and he could hear, above their straining laughs
the rustling foolscap of their epitaphs.

THE POET AS MASTERCRAFTSMAN

Eras do not end when great poets die,
for poetry is not whole: it is where man
chose mountains to conform, to carve his own
face among the Gothic richness and the sky:
and the gargoyles: and the lesser tradesmen.
Praise from the apprentice is always shown
in miniatures of a similar stone.
I saw the master in his human guise
open doors to let me in, and rhythm out:
he smiled and entertained into the night.
I was aware of work undone: his eyes
like owls, warned images from the room.
Under the stairs the muse was crying: shields
clashed in the kitchen and the war drum's boom:
men in celtic war dress entered from the right.
I left, my conversation put to rout.

To poets peace poetry never yields.

THE POET AS BLACK SHEEP

I have seen him dine
in middle-class surroundings
his manners refined,
as his family around him
talk about nothing,
one of their favourite theses.

I have seen him lying
between the street and pavement,
atoning, dying
for their sins: the fittest payment
he can make for them:
to get drunk and go to pieces.

On his father's face
in sparse lines etched out by ice,
the puritan race
has come to its zenith of grey spite,
its climax of hate,
its essence of frigidity.

Let the bourgeoise beware,
who could not control his head
and kept it in their care
until the brain bled:
this head is a poet's head,
this head holds a galaxy.

THE PERSON NOX AGONISTES

Every rural cage has prisoners,
every small hill-sheltered townland,
every whitewashed tourist'd village
holds a heart that cannot speak out,
lives a life of angered murmurs.
Over eleven pints of Guinness,
over fifty bitter Woodbines,
we have talked about our futures:
we have found no quick solution.

If one is lax in adoration,
still the priests have satisfaction
by our appearance every Sunday.
If to small tyrant employers
we bring the benefit of Unions
we are unemployed eccentrics.

If what we love is all corruption,
we must sacrifice our reason,
we must sit here in this townland
talking always of the future,
finding out no quick solutions,
over eleven pints of Guinness,
over fifty bitter Woodbines.

THE POET AS WOMAN OF IRELAND

This woman whose dowry was doom
went to a loveless land:
her fragile face enslaved the race
to whom she stretched her hand.
They played fine music at her house
and danced until the dawn:
unquivered the dart to find the heart
of that harmless white fawn.
This woman whose dowry was death
sang their requiem
and hollow bones made the organ's tones
sweet as birdsong to them,
I brought the white flower in spring,
soon the autumn fruit,
with her white ire and her red fire
she killed it at the root.
This woman whose dowry is love
she sang her ancient songs:
the ardent throngs beat brazen gongs
which she is mistress of.
This woman whose dowry is song
came home to her own place
her Irish tongue to sing among
her own ungrateful race.

THE PERSON AS DREAMER:
WE TALK ABOUT THE FUTURE

. . . it has to be a hill,
high, of course, and twilit.
There have to be some birds,
all sadly audible:
a necessary haze,
and small wristlets of rain:
yes, and a tremendous
air of satisfaction.
Both of us shall be old
and both our wives, of course,
had died, young, and tragic.
And all our children have
gone their far ways, estranged,
or else not begotten.
We have been through a war,
been hungry, and heroes:
and here we are now, calm,
fed, and reminiscent.
The hills are old, silent:
our pipe-smoke rises up.
We have come a long way . . .

THE PERSON AS SPIRIT OF
THE RIVER

My first druid of nature,
lone man knowing music of
curlew, whistle of otter,
taught me the river and love
of the fish: lone man in small
southern town, I saw your eyes
mild as mist: took as symbols
your animals: gulls that rise
up screaming in the inland,
crow of cock pheasant, long and
copper to my ears, after
your describing them: your hands
from feather, bone and fire wire
fashioning the flies to fish
just wanting from me the truth
and may God grant you your wish.

In the bright night of two moons,
moon on water, moon on tree,
back from the devious ways
of poetry, hail to me.
In the bright night of two moons
at musical riverbends
we shall pray that there may be
no deserting between friends.

THE POET DREAMS AND
RESOLVES

To be alone, and not to be lonely:
To have time to myself, and not be bored:
To live in some house suburban, beside
The mountains, with an adequate supply
Of stout and spirits (or of stout only)
And some cigarettes, and writing paper,
And a little cheap food and a small hoard
Of necessary books: where I could write
In dark as monks did, with only blue sky
As interference, wind as soul-reaper.

But what would I do if on certain nights
I was mad in heat for the public lights?
I would chain myself to a living tree
To foil the Sirens of the distant city.

THE POET AS EXILE

In a Roman beer-house
we forsaw
we had little time.
We had to ply two trades,
trade of work, trade of rhyme,
both unfinished when we slept.

There were
picture-postcards of the streets
for sale
under the deathroom of John Keats:
here Caesar fell,
here hot chestnuts are for sale.

In a Roman beer-house
we had talked,
no answer found, unless
we had outlived our usefulness
and no dignity had kept.

By the fountains of Rome
we sat down and wept.

VIII: Sonnets from the dark side of the Mind 1972
(for John Cussen)

1

I have been stone, dust of space, sea and sphere:
flamed in the supernova before man
or manmade gods made claim to have shaped me.
I have always been, will always be: I
am a pinch of earth compressed in the span
of a snail-shell: galaxies' energy,
the centre of the sun, the arch of sky:
I became all that all things ever can.
I *will* be here: I have always been here.
Buddha had to walk upon me: my snows
were not so kind, my ice was sharp as grass.
Upon me, even Christ encountered fear:
the nails were mine, the mallet mine, the blows
were mine. *I* grew the tree that grew the cross.

2

I am not free. I am bound by bread
to concrete chariots. My time is sold
for smallest coin, my acreage for beads.
The injury my freedom brings on heads
that are bound to me, that must always hold
on to me, because their essential needs
are love, and warmth, and bread, or seem to be,
is worth no walking on the mountains. Dread
is a bat ears never grow old to: sun
glorious on choral mornings can hear
it demand the insidious oarsman's fee.
I cannot go walk upon the mountain — run,
perhaps — but such a freedom, dogged by fear,
is just to be *one* guilt-edged morning free.

3

We can foretell the rising tide, the green
time of the wheat's nipple: we are not men.
Smiths, to your gold — carvers, to your agate.
we are men who are men, must not be seen
as men: make masks, make signs. Scribe, to your pen —
wonders, murders, myths and comets now relate.
The people's waiting eye begs for its hood
and will contemplate no magnitude.
The priest is the servant of blood: no gilt
or linen, or silver, or cloth of gold
can hide the true nature of sacrifice:
bread broke is bone broke, wine spilt is blood spilt,
bell is brazen gong. We, who once had souls
are now encased in pillared naves of ice.

4

Again, the coming round of time, the War
Of life become at last jeux d'Hecatombe:
The sudden herald of the blazing star
Into the piebald world will certain come.

After the twenty-seventh year, black popes
Will make an exile of the final Man,
Girded with satin, Satan and straw ropes
Flogged from the dungeons of the Vatican.

Who is this Christ, that he should challenge Paul?
What is this monster from the Middle Sea?
An invented state will have conquered all
And the Gentile feel the whips of Jewry.

With her vicious eyes slit in light, the cat
Expands like fungus in her habitat.

5

Something is blesséd. I can tell my mind,
Show all the small parlours, all the wide rooms:
Façades much rebuilt on and hid behind
Dilapidated sheds and family tombs.

Something is blesséd. I can sell my soul,
A guinea or a penn'orth: it resumes
Its place, and bargained for again is still whole.

Times it can be reckoned, if gold, in troy —
Fine grains of love, filings of gentleness.
Or if sour black earth, in avoirdupois —
Whipping itself to hate when under stress.

The word is brain, made flesh to hold debate.
The very cells of hunger saying yes:
But the poem is the heart, incarnate.

· 6

Polyzoic demon, in truth thou art
Dark Asmodeus: teach me what I lack,
The secret of another human heart.

Teach me, the Circle of the Zodiac,
To scale the wall that keeps a man alone,
The method of compassionate attack:

Help me design *tormenta* that would stone
All the social ramparts round a mine
Or how to take the marrow from the bone

Or help me by some wise device to find
The soul's armour's single elusive crack
Or press me keys that silence will unbind —

Why I called demons with my magic rods?
I got no satisfaction from the gods.

7

A haphazard blue fire as Phoebus dies:
O sleep with Phoebus till the fight is won,
For he may die, but day will certain come.
What is this blue stone, kindred to the skies?
As ring of gold is brother to the sun,
As music is magic the gold bees hum.

With hunchback of dark the dead night defies,
Its silver eyes spy from their blackened lairs:

The soul hides in the womb and in the flesh,
Hides its terror in pleasure, safe awhile
From the silkwhite, carnivorous mares
Which the pure unphysical mind enmesh
Who led by a holy angelic smile,
Turns from the body to the claws of bears.

8

Take this salve, Pamphila, oil of ages,
Pomade that eluded many sages —
Many half in love with sin and half with love,
Afraid to sacrifice a useless dove,
To sprinkle blood or to invert the Cross,
Afraid that any gain might be a loss.
Sweet Pamphila, all sacrifice is kin,
And Christ is used to catch the snake within:
Shapes in visitation to the crystal glass
Haunt the crypt and nave through the Pauline Mass.
Is blood of man, though God, more sweet in smell
Than spilt blood of a sinless cockerel?

Pamphila, take this salve: be brave, be bold —
All this knowledge for one piece of gold?

9

I saw magic on a green country road —
That old woman, a bag of sticks her load,

Blackly down to her thin feet a fringed shawl,
A rosary of bone on her horned hand,
A flight of curlews scribing by her head,
And ashtrees combing with their frills her hair.

Her eyes, wet sunken holes pierced by an awl,
Must have deciphered her adoring land:
And curlews, no longer lean birds, instead
Become ten scarlet comets in the air.

Some incantation from her canyoned mouth,
Irish, English, blew frost along the ground,
And even though the wind was from the South
The ashleaves froze without an ashleaf sound.

10

A soft internal music of his own
Played on his dead lips. His dead face was pale
And his dead eyes like almond-cuts in stone,
His nostrils gilt and sunk as Holy Grail.

And linen sheet and marble slab must bear
This fine body and black basaltic hair

A night in chapel and in father's house
Before the day and happy burial.
He was a soldier of the Golden Rose

And will embrace in earth the Holy Spouse
And end his sensual questing after all
In calm, erotic and profound repose.

He was a soldier of the Human War
For his few years, a perfect avatar.

11

To the vulgar speak only vulgar things:
For I have found the soul of this foul world:
God's breath lodged in a shell becomes impearled
And set into my sceptre and my rings.

I was the king of that ancient country
Who tried to embrace the Mother of God,
Bluerobed and gold, enamelled and moon beshod:
I am ash for my mad effrontery.

They give us demons to impregnate them
But lust for Good must die inside the soul
Where mere angels are prostitutes unpriced.

So must I do with Mother Mary's hem
And die now, lost, but holy and unwhole,
Forbid to kiss the lips of Jesus Christ?

12

Here be the burnings, all for wizardry,
Done by the Bisop of Würzburg city:

The steward of the Senate, name Gering,
Senator Bannach, fattest man in town,
And Goebel's child, a girl most beautiful:
Silberhans, a minstrel awandering,
And a blind girl whose skin was very brown,
And a student, new from the Music School.

Liebler's daughter: Madame Knertz: Schwartz a priest –
Nor was the innkeeper of Klingen released.
Walkenberger's little daughter, at home
Was executed, burnt outside her door:

Also some travellers going to Rome,
And Ehling a vicar, and many more.

13

Lamp-light makes all trees circular, in streets
Where nymph and spirit never live and sing:
In Dublin town, this is a miracle.
Who has not seen this vision has no love,
Is surely urban as a house of glass —
The tree adore the sun within the lamp,
The tree attempt a dryad of its own.

Busy men build glaciers and the soul retreats,
Dies, as blackbarred wasps after their own sting,
In its small ivory winding of shell.
And weakly, velvet fist in velvet glove,
The heart is jammed at the vacant bypass
And trees conjure religion in the damp
In Dublin streets, cemented and alone.

SECULAR PRAYERS

to look at lovely things and not be dumb,
to cry and not be wordless, to praise
the relics, the remains
the last insignia of God
in this,
the second mesozoic age

*

whom I ask for no gift
whom I thank for all things,
this is the morning.
night is gone, a dawn
comes up in birds and sounds of the city.
there will be light
to live by, things
to see: my eyes will lift
to where the sun in vermillion sits,
and I will love and have pity.

*

you are alive at last
to the discovery
of land, to know the ways
of cities and forget
the ways of birds. I wish
you grief in the concrete
galleries: but no grief
beside the cliffs of some
atlantic town, no grief
at nightfall to count stars:
only grief where man builds,
only grief in the city.

*

pray time, for the man
from the soft inland:
(there is the sea, up
in parabolas
of foam, above the
rocks: the town in
nestling limestone under
wing, the smell of
the very cavities
of earth, a smell
of women, and cold
dead things) sea-sailor.

*

now the delicate
notes of wheat blow through
the harrowed earth,
this is the spring,
and so many flowers
walk the land in
resurrection,
and the filaments
of dead birds' bones
shine,
embossed like ivory
on the road.

*

I am glad for the frost,
leaves of exotic line
by ice on glass,
a bitter cold
and trees made ghost
by flashes of light
from facets of icicle,
and crystalline,
the animal tracks.

I am glad for the snow,
it is a white bird frantic,
a flight of white moths,
water frozen to intracacies:
and in the blinding neutral lull
all the ways, made beautiful.
and for this animal wind
loose in the talking houses
I am glad, and in its will
bending the imperturable,
the tree, the tower
the turret of antiquity,
or quiet exhalations from bird's wings

I am glad for the rain,
in its steel and distant parallels
on the square-cut leaf-thin
rectangles
the quarried slate on houses,
in its death-willingness
its descent, its million
feet of birds across town-houses.

for thunder, its talking on close days
is its prayer: packice calves,
there is a fall of rock:
it barks like dogs of god,
talks in tongues of fire:
deadly.
and electric.

and for the sun
will there ever be
an end of ceremony?
there is no more glory
hawkskilled eye can see
in the enterprise of night
the clouds of milk,
the silver bees,
than a simple coming on of day.

*

hot the hanging apple,
the dusty bodies walk
the town, in neurotic
sweat: for summer I give
thanks. rivers are white with cool
and nothing sings: it is
the true gestation.
there is a flight of seeds
across an open place,
o hot the hanging apple.

*

"Amid the broken rocks
— shall we stay here
with the wild hawks?
— no, ere the hot noon come
dive we down — safe:"
We will be here
with the wild hawks
when our intelligent
friend talks
to tell us of
his grief at ours.
we will not be safe.

*

I will love you
till you loving cease:
there will be no
more bargain in our lives.
we will not wear
the costumes of pretence:
you will love me
till my loving cease.
no act one, scene one
in our lives: you
will say the truth to me,
and not castrate
the brevity of love
in tense
neurotic silences.

*

there is surfeit of fungi
from the wet ground
in a moist luminosity
and a noise of pheasants
under fern:
fruit in scarlet complexes
on haw and dogrose:
toxic slime on fungus
stalks and the sleep-scented
pall of the autumn ash.
all things age,
all things are harvest
to themselves.

*

distance, and absence,
pares this oak of an
old remembrance down
to fragile lines of
nudity: there is
time, in guise of flesh
and long hair, there, by
me, now old from you
in new and eager
arms: but here, in new
and eager arms, I
do not shut you out.
I have loved you:
there is none more beautiful.

*

whom I ask for no gift
whom I thank for all things,
down a tenuous dimension
I descend where all things
wild, the barking fox,
the wolf by grave, the ghosts
of dead, descend
and bodies longed for
in a fraction of the mind
are supine by wild ferns.
call here, wild eyes:
and I will wake
to the light to live by.
or will not wake,
but in a gentle trauma die.

*

black frost, pike locked
below the ice,
the winter season.
I give thanks for life
among these dead,
the bony men of trees
and the leaves along
the road, like the webbed
feet of dead
waterfowl:
the winter season,
the pike locked
below the ice.

*

what was not human
though from womb of woman,
for this a small grief.
for whom forced a love
on you, will have to be
the necessary funeral,
the necessary grief
for you, already
skeletal, you have sinned
by forcing years of
faithfulness from us,
die now, rest: let us rest,
there will be valid
human grief for all
these deaths: the heart will love
all it has to love.

*

whom I ask for no gift
whom I thank for all things,
there is a setting of the sun,
and a coming on of dark
and the familiar stars,
and then the moon runs
crescent into clouds,
and all things but the night things
merge in their violet sleep.

*

o in this human city
there is only a human
season, concealed from my face,
hid frequency of birth,
the young in their concrete schools,
age forbidden to the flesh,
the dead in surburban cemeteries.
for me there are no seasons,
no coming of flower, or fall
of leaf: nor is there soft summer,
and the winter is mere rain,
and I adore them in their distance
for from the highest oblong house,
there is some intimation of the hills.

IX: The Retreat of Ita Cagney
(for Liam Brady)

1

Their barbarisim did not assuage the grief:
their polished boots, their Sunday clothes,
the drone of hoarse melodeons.
The smoke was like the edge of blue scythes.
The downpour smell of overcoats
made the kitchen cry for air:
snuff lashed the nose like nettles
and the toothless praising of the dead
spun on like unoiled bellows.
She could not understand her grief:
the women who had washed his corpse
were now more intimate with him
than she had ever been.
She put a square of silk upon her head
and hidden in the collars of her coat
she felt her way along the white-washed walls.
The road became a dim knife.
She had no plan
but instinct neighed around her
like a pulling horse.

2

Moulded to a wedge of jet
by the wet night, her black hair
showed one grey rib, like a fine
steel filing on a forge floor.
One deep line, cut by silent
days of hate in the expanse
of sallow skin above her brows,
dipped down to a tragic slant.
Her eyebrows were thin penlines
finely drawn on parchment sheets,
hair after miniscule hair
a linear masterpiece.
Triangles of minute gold
broke her open blue of eyes
that had looked on bespoke love,
seeing only to despise.

Her long nose was almost bone
making her face too severe:
the tight and rose-edged nostrils
never belled into a flare.
A fine gold down above the
upper lip did not maintain
its prettiness nor lower's swell
make it less a graph of pain.
Chin and jawline delicate,
neither weak nor skeletal:
bone in definite stern mould,
small and strong like a fox-skull.
Her throat showed no signs of age.
no sinews reinforced flesh
or gathered in clenched fistfuls
to pull skin to lined mesh.

The rest was shapeless, in black woollen dress.

Door opened halving darkness bronze
and half an outlined man
filled half the bronze.
Lamplight whipped upright into gold
the hairs along his nose,
poured coils of honey
around his head.
In the centre of his throat
clipped on his blue-striped shirt
a stud briefly pierced a thorn of light.
The male smell of the kitchen
engulfed her face,
odours of lost gristle
and grease along the wall:
her headscarf laughed a challenge
its crimson wrinkles crackling.
He knuckled up the wooden latch
and closed the door for many years.

4

Great ceremony later causes pain:
next year in hatred and in grief, the vain
white dress, the bulging priest, the frantic dance,
the vowing and the sickening wishes, land
like careful hammers on a broken hand.
But in this house no sacred text was read.
He offered her some food: they went to bed,
his arm and side a helmet for her head.
This was no furtive country coupling: this
was the ultimate hello, kiss and kiss
exchanged and bodies introduced: their sin
to choose so late a moment to begin
while shamefaced chalice, pyx, ciborium
clanged their giltwrapped anger in the room.

5

The swollen leather creaks
like lost birds
and the edges of her shawl
fringe down into the dark
while glaciers of oilskins drip around her
and musical traces and chafing of harness
and tedious drumming of hooves on the gravel
make her labour pains become
the direct rebuke and pummel of the town.
Withdrawing from her pain
to the nightmare warmth
beneath her shawl
the secret meeting in the dark
becomes a public spectacle
and baleful sextons turn their heads
and sullen shadows mutter hate
and snarl and debate
and shout vague threats of hell.

The crossroads blink their headlamp warning
and break into a rainbow on the shining tar:
the new skull turns in its warm pain,
the new skull pushes towards its morning.

6

O my small and warm creature
with your gold hair and your skin
that smells of milk and apples,
I must always lock you in
where nothing much can happen.
But you will hate these few rooms,
for a dove is bound to come
with leaves and outdoor perfumes:
already the talons drum
a beckoning through the slates,
bringing from the people words
and messages of hate.
Soon the wingbeats of this bird
will whisper down in their dive:
I dread the coming of this dove
for its beak will be a knife
and if you leave armed with my love
they will tell you what you lack:
they will make you wear my life
like a hump upon your back.

. . . each footprint being green in the wet grass
in search of mushrooms like white moons of lime,
each hazel ooze of cowdung through the toes,
being warm, and slipping like a floor of silk . . .
but all the windows are in mourning here:
the giant eye gleams like a mucous hill.
She pictured cowslips, then his farmer's face,
and waited in a patient discontent.
A heel of mud fell from his garden boots
embossed with nails and white-hilt shoots of grass
a hive of hayseeds in the woollen grooves
of meadow-coats fell golden on the floor,
and apples with medallions of rust
englobed a thickening cider on the shelf:
and holly on the varnished frames bent in
and curved its catsharp fingernails of green.
The rooms became resplendent with these signs.

8

I will put purple crepe and crimson crepe
and white crepe on the shelf
and watch the candles cry
o salutaris hostia.
I will light the oil lamp till it burns
like a scarlet apple
and watch the candlegrease
upon the ledges interweave
to ropes of ivory.
I have not insulted God:
I have insulted
crombie coats and lace mantillas
sunday best and church collections
and they declare my life a sinful act:
not because it hurts
the God they say they love —
but because my happiness
is not a public fact.

In rhythmic dance the neighbours move
outside the door: become dull dolls
as venom breaks in strident fragments
on the glass: broken insults clatter
on the slates: the pack retreats,
the instruments of siege withdraw
and skulk into the foothills to regroup.
The houses nudge and mutter through the night
and wait intently for the keep to fall.
She guards her sleeping citizen
and paces the exhausting floor:
on the speaking avenue of stones
she hears the infantry of eyes advance.

X: A Farewell to English

THE BUFFETING
(for Healy and Broderick)

1

What did I wake up to
but a bubbling trachea,
the drug inlaid upon my inner throat
like the roughest texture:
looked at the slim tobacco
in a rage and inlaid more.
I walked to the motorcar
and moved out through
a tedious range of colours.
Speed almost equals exhilaration:
but this is not the truth:
my organs, vessels, lungs
moved merely at a faster rate,
the tedious range of colours
merged more rapidly,
became an overlap of sights,
moved more rapidly to slowing down
to weariness, to total ruin.

2

And so the spectrum dwindled down
became a static and a separate
demonstration:
the puce, the black, the military grey.
Spittle seemed to reach
an unaccountable proportion,
the odour of cracks upon the glass,
the noise of many windows shattering.

I sat down there,
huddling my broken innards,
looking at points I barely focused on,
the puce, the black, the military grey,
miles from my face
too converse and in contrast
to be part of any harmony.
But I was here for some reason:
there was some meaning in this disintegration,
some old meaning.

3

I left the car.
The furthest points were colossi of sense:
my spine became erect
and lifted fistfulls of my softest part
up and forward into some array.
But then the lungs snapped shut
commanded by some master sinew
and the heart became a ball of pain,
the target of some vicious nail:
and that buffeting began.
Eardrums toppled as if the air had fists:
breath was forced backwards by the blows:
head swung left: right: up: down:
like a frightened door:
heart noisily became a metronome.
Angry and insulting, I withdrew,
left the paltry habitat of the beast
and recovered in the clinic comfort
of the car.

4

That night
I crouched in a small alcove of heat
under a rough cloth rubbed hard
by years of limbs shivering,
recycling the same breath,
the same comforting smells.
I had escaped the bastinado.
But only for a while.
The sashes buckled
and the violent night
demanded entry: the drums
beseeched and screamed.
The gables cowered like a broken man:
and the pummeling insisted.
I screamed. I prayed to my forsaken gods.
But nothing stopped.
All night it fell upon the glass
like an angry couple
in another room.

STRUTS
(for Paul Durcan)

We are all spread out upon a hill,
each to his ledge,
visibly almost nil,
seldom seeing each other —
hearing an occasional shout
above or below
and sometimes and most welcome,
seeing fires like silver spirals
jump along the crevices.
We are climbing upwards into time
and climbing backwards into tradition,
the sudden message on a rope
evoking the cosiness of soft-lit rooms,
the comfort and the smell
of sharing ancient overcoats.
Sometimes a rope gives,
implodes unweighted in the hand,
and then tradition, time and fire
mix in a spinning blur:
the hill unskins the knuckles.

Miles, to the obscurity of some pelmet
cloth drags its oscillations.
Sitting here: for hours:
venturing sometimes to the concrete inclines:
sometimes climbing up
to where   is between me and the light
or dark or green blurs or white blurs
but not getting beyond it:
sometimes falling down the slope
but feeling no pain.
Just lying beside jute sacks among the grooves,
lying beside the giant flakes of paint.

Then there was that crack:
like a light bulb violently blowing;
And an undesignable shape
— seemingly three-dimensional —
appeared between me and the light,
comparable to no familiar symbol.
It almost named itself.
But I could put no name on it.

HORSE BREAKING LOOSE

I was very young
and spirals of brown dust
broke into chaos on my sandals
and a long cone of white
tapered away to a line,
hot among dark edges,
walled by massive growths
of unfinished green.
At the apex of the cone
a figure like a smudge of rust
snapped into a violent smoke,
its black besoldiered
by a piping of black froth
and velvet pistons pounded into fear
and pieces of the road fell off
and fell disintegrating sparks.
All this violence and men running passed me by
with lashing whips of wire
and long outlandish coats
with voice and weapons most barbarous and uncouth.
I fell into a green and giving mass
and sweat performed a sickle on my face.

EARLY ONE MORNING

There was nothing there
but the darkness and myself: ·
then slowly out of sleep
my eyes pulled me,
needled by a speck of lead dust.
No one else had thrust
a limb out of the headless
shadows of themselves:
I could see them stacked
on their beds.
At last I was the first.
A grey fingerprint
embossed my eye.
I knew I had something to say.
I began to cry.
A slow bubble of grey spread:
every shadow grew a head,
every shadow began to shout.
Then a film of blood
seemed to coat all things
and I was loudest of all beings
though my cry had lost its meaning.
A fan of silver
underglowed the blood:
we stared at each other,
none being understood
and grey and red and silver
washed the world
louder and more clear
than all our noise.

USA

They who were once proud of their persuasion
now in their declining jaws grow small bones,
their teeth grow huge, their skins turn yellow and
crack. They are slowly becoming Asian,
Apache arrows in their chromosomes.
They killed her lovers, expecting to replace
pure blood with their dubious bastard stocks,
using the weapons of civilized man:
bad alcohol and God, guns and small-pox.
Dogs with the right to bear arms would found
a juster republic.
                    Why are they afraid?
They live upon a burial ground:
Latin, Anglo-Saxon, Teuton, Celt and Jew
avert their eyes, afraid to look around
and see ghosts of Navaho, Cheyenne and Sioux.
They chained the land and pulled her down
and nailed her to the sea with towns.
She lies on her back, her belly cut in fields
of red and yellow earth. She does not yield,
she is not theirs. She does not love this race.
She will not open her legs to enclose
the scum of Europe, jockeying for grace.

THE OAT WOMAN

She heard the gates of autumn
    splinter into ash
grey shock of toppling insects
    as the gate broke down.
Old nails in their nests of rust
    screamed at this swivel:
booted limbs of working men
    walked on her body.
Their coats lay down in sculpture,
    each with a tired dog:
thin blades quaked at blunt whetstones:
    purple barked at blue.
The whetstones drank their water
    and flayed the bright edge.
Each oat like sequin shivered:
    her gold body tensed,
fear lapped across her acre
    in a honey wave
and buckets of still porter
    turned to discs of black.
Iron and stone called warning
    to her shaking ears:
arms enforced a fierce caress,
    brown and blind and bronze.
Sickles drover her back and back
    to a golden wedge:
her hissing beads fell silent
    in dead yellow bands.
Across her waist the reaping
    whipped like silver moons,
wind whistled banked flute laments,
    musical sweat fell.
Animals left in terror
    pheasant, sparrow, hare
deserting her in anguish,
    crowding from her skirts.

She curled in a golden fear
     on the last headland,
the sad outline of her breats
     bare through the oatstalks.
Four arms took sickles and swung —
     no single killer:
she vanished from the shorn field
     in that red autumn.

PIGKILLING

Like a knife cutting a knife
his last plea for life
echoes joyfully in Camas.
An egg floats
like a navel
in the pickling-barrel:
before he sinks,
his smiling head
sees a delicate girl
up to her elbows
in a tub of blood
while the avalanche
of his offal steams
among the snapping dogs
and mud
and porksteaks
coil in basins
like bright snakes
and buckets of boiling water hiss
to soften his bristles
for the blade.
I kicked his golden bladder
in the air.
. It landed like a moon
among the damsons.
Like a knife cutting a knife
his last plea for life
echoed joyfully in Camas.

Camas: a townland five miles south of
Newcastle West in Co. Limerick where
I spent most of my childhood.

THE HORSE CATCHER

Here was the river of our youth, browned by
bog in far-off uplands, the green hedges
crushing puffs of meadow-sweet to the brink
of the water, the swallows overjoyed
at the new summer, the rats in silver
that swam across, the stoat in his waistcoat
eeled on the bank, and the stones were restless.
Pencilling their electric lines, plying
their blue wool, the kingfishers webbed the span:
the hooked trout jumped up; flicked his silver sickle.

Winkers and wet rope in hand, his hawk's eyes
blinking on their secrets, he left green footprints
in the white dew.
    White horse, my holy anguish
tumbles like tambourines: it has no name.
Sin has no name in this townland: some men
have faults. Nested in green gloves, I slit the golden
throats of all the morning's dandelions,
and I wait in ambush.
    Christ on His Cross
holds out no hope for me: Mary in blue
and gold will not crush me like the serpent.
I tell them over again: forgive me
for what I am, but I am nothing else.
And the Church, inside, smells like unvarnished˙
boxes.
   Older than we are now and more
shrunken, not so brown and with fewer fish,
the river eats its red-earth banks like an
hourglass sand: it has uncovered a limestone
bed and cut a slow groove in the yellow mud
deeper than eels ever dreamed it could.
His body is there, Christ around his neck
for stone, his limbs white as water, his hawk's
eyes open on his secrets, soul at rest.

THE PERPETUAL MOMENT
(for Lara)

I have looked into the jackdaws'
nest, ignoring their wild caws
to see a thing that always was.

I have looked at the pike's spiked jaws,
at the pads on foxes' paws,
to see a things that always was.

I have looked at ice as it thaws
from the red beads of late haws
to see a thing that always was.

I have looked at fledglings' maws,
the delicacy of rats' claws,
to see a thing that always was.

I have looked for flaws
and found many: because
I am not content
to see a thing untouched
that always was.

STAGHORN WHISTLE
(for the Grahams)

1

Man bundled in his frozen coats
cracked his fingers back to life
from his staghorn whistle
sucked a plug of ice
and shrilled a note.
I could see its blue parabola
drop where dog and sheep
smoked white in the grey air.

2

My uncle ran away from school
blue and free in a sailor suit:
the country heard his whistle blaring
pea berling in its spitfilled chamber.

3

I sit bewildered by machines
the lights and coils conveying
messages for morons
three inches of rough staghorn whistle
in my hand, a leaping frieze
of man and dog and mountain
my uncle dancing in the fields
and two gold girls in a morning stream.

PUBLIC SERVANT
(for Dan McMahon)

Here, where men sit down to die
In pensioned, taxed anonymity
And who at sixty-five retire
No longer worthy of their hire
And in a sad funeral mime
Are given clocks to count their time
To show how much of life they paid
To the cannibalistic State
I sit among the beaten ranks
For meagre pay, for meagre thanks,
And fawn on those who once did fawn
On toads of bureaucratic spawn
The holy rule in here is "ask"
A painful and belittling task;
But before I clear my throat
I hang my soul up with my coat
A perfect cog, conformed to plan
But really only half a man
Whose soul hangs quietly in the gloom
Of the downstairs locker-room.

THE POSSIBILITY THAT HAS BEEN
OVERLOOKED IS THE FUTURE

I look along the valley of my gun.
An otter examines the air,
silver in the sun.
I have hunted him for many days.
I will not kill him where he stands:
double death in the beeches
demands he be given a chance.
I take stock, warm metal in my hands.
Will he swim upstream
water from his nose a bright arrowhead?
Will he swin downstream
coiling in bubbles to the riverbed?
Will he swim cross-stream,
where an ashtree's roots are naked?
There is a chance he will swim towards me.
Will he take it?

SALLY GAP

It was left upon the granite cliff
like a discarded afterbirth:
not falling, at this distance
but like a fan of stiff
frost crashlanded.

It hung upon a cross of furze,
white like a waterfall,
moving, at this distance,
it meshes bleached,
like a lost scarf of lace.

DEATH BY THE SANTRY RIVER

From her fabric bed the nylon sheets
cascade, gritting their electric teeth,
and fall on vinyl. The clock clicks alarm
and her irritated orloned arm
reaches for a switch. Her feet slip in
to nylon, puffed and feminine:
she sips a liquid vitamin.
She sparks an orlon nightdress to the floor:
chemical solutions clean her pores.
She dons more nylon, does her hair,
fixing down each segment with a spray,
non-toxic, not to be exposed to flame.
She leaves with plastic bag and shoes
the safety of her airconditioned mews
and taps a plastic sound
across uncultivated ground

for green bracelets,
bindweed tendrils mongreled at her heels,
like bronzed bracelets greened by rain:
briars bounded in green loops,
lust on their thorntips:
white bugles blew obscene advance,
tendrils pulled her down
and grasses stabbed:
quivers of rush enter her wet mouth,
needling through the red muscle of her cheeks:
she's down:
a broken heel sticks dead
a black mushroom in the mud
swiftly to every orifice goosegrass claws
an avalanche of burrs descends her neck
burdock leech her throat like puffs of pain
hawthorn javelins poise in ranks
uncurling fernheads push aside her nipples
thistles explode inside her womb
red syllables of froth bloom from her lips:
she dies in shrouds of thistledown,
wrapped in this violent jewelry.

DRYAD

Walking in our public places,
seeing the latest art
made from the latest materials
is like finding words like "dryad"
shattered from their plinths,
statues without squares
broken marble heads of beasts:
commas of culture left
and culture lost in this city of the warehouse.

Here is a figure in metallic foil
its forty-three filaments or coils
in a perpetual tremble.
Not beautiful, not useful
but the image was the maker's own:
perhpas he heard his soul
crying outside our ramparts
or honking at a vacant by-pass.

When our neon lights drop bluely
from the warehouse windowglass
the smoky rain sneaks down the walls
the figure in metallic foil
attempts a dryad of its own
takes the time-encrusted light
as its central soul
from which the broken circles spin.

Who cannot see this vision has no love —
dryad
and her attendant ghosts
caught in the pointless barbs
of the metallic foil.

THE FINAL RENDEZVOUS

Black frost hammered the ground hard
cutting graveyard trees to shapes
of flat tin, studding the thorns
with spurs and horns of white grace.
Prongs of grass with iron root
snapped underfoot like small bones
and a white smoke of grief bound
mourners in a owl-soft tone.
Lovely, presenting a pale
face, pallor of ship and train,
her daughter and my love
watched the shovel-handle break
as obstinate ground made room,
toppling eardrums full of sea,
and unpolished-plum-dull eyes
searching for a sullen grief.
She saw me, and saw, before
heart's door opened up in pain,
love-sending eyes: then she knew
her true emotion was rage.
Ice fell as the yew's spine snapped.
Ice fell as the yew's spine snapped.

THEORY
(for Rosemary)

By glass engraved with Rousseau jungles
by frost and its momentary ferns
an old music from some other place
runs, like milk on marble tables —
a phrasing from the stellar sound,
the pure monoword:
one poem writing a book of poets.
And when this sound becomes emotion
that is the moment when the god descends.
and when the clever trap of style
snaps through the costume
its brings out the bone,
the image no mirror ever brings to bay,
the single syllable explosion.
When this emotion becomes sound
that is the moment when the god descends.

A VISIT TO CASTLETOWN HOUSE
(for Nora Graham)

The avenue was green and long, and green
light pooled under the fernheads; a jade screen
could not let such liquid light in, a sea
at its greenest self could not pretend to be
so emerald. Men had made this landscape
from a mere secreting wood: knuckles bled
and bones broke to make this awning drape
a fitting silk upon its owner's head.

The house was lifted by two pillared wings
out of its bulk of solid chisellings
and flashed across the chestnut-marshalled lawn
a few lit windows on a bullock bawn.
The one-way windows of the empty rooms
reflected meadows, now the haunt
of waterbirds: where hawtrees were in bloom,
and belladonna, a poisonous plant.

A newer gentry in their quaint attire
looked at maps depicting alien shire
and city, town and fort: they were his seed,
that native who had taken coloured beads
disguised as chandeliers of vulgar glass
and made a room to suit a tasteless man
— a graceful art come to a sorry pass —
painted like some demented tinker's van.

But the music that was played in there —
that had grace, a nervous grace laid bare,
Tortellier unravelling sonatas
pummelling the instrument that has
the deep luxurious sensual sound,
allowing it no richness, making stars
where moons would be, choosing to expound
music as passionate as guitars.

I went into the calmer, gentler hall
in the wineglassed, chattering interval:
there was the smell of rose and woodsmoke there.
I stepped into the gentler evening air
and saw black figures dancing on the lawn,
Eviction, Droit de Seigneur, Broken Bones:
and heard the crack of ligaments being torn
and smelled the clinging blood upon the stones.

MRS HALPIN AND THE LIGHTNING

When thunder entered like an easter priest
and draped its purple on Mullach a'Radhairc
a horse took fright and broke its neck
against a pierstone:
the carshafts gave like small bones
and the tilted wheel spun.
When the blue sheets crackled
with electric starch
Mrs Halpin with a goose's wing
flailed holy water drops
like the steel tips of holy whips
to beat the demons from the room.
But they would not go away.
Their garments shook her rosary
as they danced on the stone floor.
Her fear was not the simple fear of one
who does not know the source of thunder:
these were the ancient Irish gods
she had deserted for the sake of Christ.
They waited in the earth and sky
to punish and destroy
their fickle congregation.
Mrs Halpin knew the reason why.

Mullach a' Radhairc: hills to the south-west of
Newcastle West.

DEATH OF AN IRISHWOMAN

Ignorant, in the sense
she ate monotonous food
and thought the world was flat,
and pagan, in the sense
she knew the things that moved
all night were neither dogs nor cats
but púcas and darkfaced men
she nevertheless had fierce pride.
But sentenced in the end
to eat thin diminishing porridge
in a stone-cold kitchen
she clenched her brittle hands
around a world
she could not understand.
I loved her from the day she died.
She was a summer dance at the crossroads.
She was a cardgame where a nose was broken.
She was a song that nobody sings.
She was a house ransacked by soldiers.
She was a language seldom spoken.
She was a child's purse, full of useless things.

A VISIT TO CROOM 1745
(for Séamus Ó Cinnéide)

The thatch dripped soot,
the sun was silver
because the sky
from ruts of mud to high blaze
was water:
white-washed walls were silver,
limeflakes opened like scissored pages
nesting moss and golds of straw
and russet pools of soot:
windows small as ratholes
shone like frost-filled hoofprints,
the door was charted
by the tracery of vermin.
Five Gaelic faces stopped their talk,
turned from the red of fire
into a cloud of rush-light fumes,
scraped their pewter mugs
across the board and talked about the king.
I had walked a long time
in the mud to hear
an avalanche of turf fall down,
fourteen miles in straw-roped overcoat
passing for Irish all along the road
now to hear a Gaelic court
talk broken English of an English king.
It was a long way
to come for nothing.

A FAREWELL TO ENGLISH
for Brendan Kennelly

1

Her eyes were coins of porter and her West
Limerick voice talked velvet in the house:
her hair was black as the glossy fireplace
wearing with grace her Sunday-night-dance best.
She cut the froth from glasses with a knife
and hammered golden whiskies on the bar
and her mountainy body tripped the gentle
mechanism of verse: the minute interlock
of word and word began, the rhythm formed.
I sunk my hands into tradition
sifting the centuries for words. This quiet
excitement was not new: emotion challenged me
to make it sayable. The clichés came
at first, like matchsticks snapping from the world
of work: mánla, séimh, dubhfholtach, álainn, caoin:
they came like grey slabs of slate breaking from
an ancient quarry, mánla, séimh, dubhfholtach,
álainn, caoin, slowly vaulting down the dark
unused escarpments, mánla, séimh, dubhfholtach,
álainn, caoin, crashing on the cogs, splinters
like axeheads damaged the wheels, clogging
the intricate machine, mánla, séimh,
dubhfholtach, álainn, caoin. Then Pegasus
pulled up, the girth broke and I was flung back
on the gravel of Anglo-Saxon.
What was I doing with these foreign words?
I, the polisher of the complex clause,
wizard of grasses and warlock of birds
midnight-oiled in the metric laws?

dubhfholtach: blacklocked. álainn: beautiful.
mánla, séimh agus caoin: words whose meanings hover about
the English adjectives graceful, gentle.

2

Half afraid to break a promise
made to Dinny Halpin Friday night
I sat down from my walk to Camas
Sunday evening, Doody's Cross,
and took off my burning boots
on a gentle bench of grass.
The cows had crushed the evening
green with mint:
springwater from the roots
of a hawkfaced firtree on my right
swamped pismires bringing home
their sweet supplies
and strawberries looked out
with ferrets' eyes.
These old men walked on the summer road
súgán belts and long black coats
with big ashplants and half-sacks
of rags and bacon on their backs.
They stopped before me with a knowing look
hungry, snotnosed, half-drunk.
I said "grand evening"
and they looked at me awhile
then took their roads
to Croom, Meentogues and Cahirmoyle.
They look back once,
black moons of misery
sickling their eye-sockets,
a thousand years of history
in their pockets.

Croom: area in Co. Limerick associated with Andrias Mac Craith (d. 1975); also, seat of the last 'courts' of Gaelic poetry; also, my birthplace.
Meentogues: birthplace of Aodhagán Ó Rathaille.
Cahirmoyle: site of the house of John Bourke (fl. 1690, patron of Dáibhí Ó Bruadair.

3

Chef Yeats, that master of the use of herbs
could raise mere stew to a glorious height,
pinch of saga, soupçon of philosophy
carefully stirred in to get the flavour right,
and cook a poem around the basic verbs.
Our commis-chefs attend and learn the trade,
bemoan the scraps of Gaelic that they know:
add to a simple Anglo-Saxon stock
Cuchulainn's marrow-bones to marinate,
a dash of Ó Rathaille simmered slow,
a glass of University hic-haec-hoc:
sniff and stand back and proudly offer you
the celebrated Anglo-Irish stew.

4

We woke one morning
in a Dublin digs
and found we were descended
from two pigs.
The brimming Irish sow
who would allow
any syphilitic boar
to make her hind-end sore
was Mammy.
Daddy was an English boar
who wanted nothing
but a sweaty rut
and ownership of any offspring.
We knew we had been robbed
but were not sure that we lost
the right to have a language
or the right to be the boss.

So we queued up at the Castle
in nineteen-twenty-two
to make our Gaelic
or our Irish dream come true.
We could have had from that start
made certain of our fate
but we chose to learn the noble art
of writing forms in triplicate.
With big wide eyes
and childish smiles
quivering on our lips
we enterered the Irish paradise
of files and paper-clips.

5

I say farewell to English verse,
to those I found in English nets:
my Lorca holding out his arms
to love the beauty of his bullets,
Pasternak who outlived Stalin
and died because of lesser beasts:
to all the poets I have loved
from Wyatt to Robert Browning:
to Father Hopkins in his crowded grave
and to our bugbear Mr. Yeats
who forced us into exile
on islands of bad verse.

Among my living friends
there is no poet I do not love,
although some write
with bitterness in their hearts:
they are one art, our many arts.
Poets with progress
make no peace or pact:
the act of poetry
is a rebel act.

6

Gaelic is the conscience of our leaders,
the memory of a mother-rape they will
not face, the heap of bloody rags they see
and scream at in their boardrooms of mock oak.
They push us towards the world of total work,
our politicians with their seedy minds
and dubious labels, Communist or
Capitalist, none wanting freedom —
only power. All that reminds us
we are human and therefore not a herd
must be concealed or killed or slowly left
to die, or microfilmed to waste no space.
For Gaelic is our final sign that
we are human, therefore not a herd.

I saw our governments the other night —
I think the scene was Leopardstown —
horribly deformed dwarfs rode the racetrack
each mounted on a horribly deformed dwarf:
greenfaced, screaming, yellow-toothed, prodding
each other with electric prods, thrashing
each others' skinny arses, dribbling snot
and smeared with their own dung, they galloped
towards the prize, a glass and concrete anus.

I think the result was a dead heat.

7

This road is not new.
I am not a maker of new things.
I cannot hew
out of the vacuumcleaner minds
the sense of serving dead kings.

I am nothing new
I am not a lonely mouth
trying to chew
a niche for culture
in the clergy-cluttered south.

But I will not see
great men go down
who walked in rags
from town to town
finding English a necessary sin
the perfect language to sell pigs in.

I have made my choice
and leave with little weeping:
I have come with meagre voice
to court the language of my people.

CORRIGENDA

page 22   line 13: The true ubermensch is the monationalist,
the raceless.

page 24   line 3: who are fathers

page 33   line 13: let your hands hold me: I am

page 114   line 25: water frozen to intricacies

page 143   line 6: to see a thing that always was

page 149   line 15 perhaps he heard his soul

page 151   line 12 it brings out the bone

INDEX OF FIRST LINES

DUE DATE

201-6503

Printed
in USA